Champagne & Caviar

Melissa Clark

Principal Photography by Bill Milne

FRIEDMAN/FAIRFAX

PUBLISHERS

A FRIEDMAN/FAIRFAX BOOK

©1999 by Michael Friedman Publishing Group, Inc.

Library of Congress Cataloging-in-Publication data available on request.

ISBN 1-56799-743-0

Principal Photographer: Bill Milne
Prop Stylist: Sylvia Lachter
Editor: Sharyn Rosart
Art Director: Jeff Batzli
Designer: Andrea Karman
Photography Director: Christopher C. Bain
Photography Editor: Wendy Missan
Production Manager: Richela Fabian
Caviar supplied by Caviarteria:
1-800-4CAVIAR or caviarteria.com

Color separations by Colourscan Overseas Co. Pte. Ltd.
Printed in China by Leefung-Asco Printers Ltd.

3 5 7 9 10 8 6 4 2

For bulk purchases and special sales, please contact:
Friedman/Fairfax Publishers
Attention: Sales Department
15 West 26th Street
New York, New York 10010
212/685-6610   FAX 212/685-1307

Visit our website:
www.metrobooks.com

SPECIAL THANKS ARE DUE TO THE MANY WHO HELPED MAKE THIS BOOK POSSIBLE.

FIRST, THERE IS MY EDITOR SHARYN ROSART, WHO CONCEIVED OF THE PROJECT, THEN NURSED IT INTO ACTUALITY. BOOK DESIGNER ANDREA KARMAN, PHOTOGRAPHER BILL MILNE, AND PHOTO EDITOR WENDY MISSAN ARE THE PEOPLE RESPONSIBLE FOR MAKING THE BOOK SO HANDSOME. FINALLY, I COULDN'T HAVE WRITTEN THIS BOOK NEARLY SO FLUIDLY IF IT WEREN'T FOR MY ASSISTANT SARA EPSTEIN, WHO LABORED ALONGSIDE ME UNTIL THE VERY END.

TO P.C.C., WITHOUT WHOM A CHAMPAGNE TOAST WOULD BE NOTHING BUT BURSTING BUBBLES.

Contents

A Sublime Experience

The first time I ate caviar, it was all about impressing the grown-ups. It was New Year's Eve, and my sister and I were eleven and twelve, respectively— finally old enough to sit at a dinner party with my parents and their gourmet friends. I piled the inky orbs high atop my toast point in frank emulation of the adults. My sister, hesitant to try new things, stuck to the known—smoked salmon—although she was a little flummoxed at the absence of bagels.

Into my mouth went the canapé, topped with a good quarter-ounce of the precious caviar, served naked but for the bread, without sour cream or onion or lemon to temper it. And I chewed … and chewed … and chewed, my mouth filling up with saliva as it attempted to diminish the horrible burst of salty fish that my adolescent palate just couldn't handle. If I hadn't been surrounded by grown-ups, desperate to be one of them, I would have spit that pernicious lump straight into my napkin.

ABOVE: Both fresh and pressed caviar are sold by the ounce in small metal tins or glass jars. If the label reads "malossol" (Russian for "little salt"), the caviar was prepared with the minimal amount of salt necessary for preservation— no more than 5% by Russian law. Malossol caviar is considered the finest. OPPOSITE: Caviar shows its rustic roots when spread in a thin layer atop a toasted slice of pumpernickel bread.

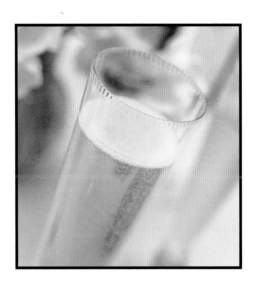

I could have rinsed my mouth out with some Champagne, but because of my age there was barely enough poured into my flute to toast the new year, let alone enough to wash down my mistake. And, while sipping that small amount of bubbling wine was infinitely more pleasurable than eating the caviar, I can't say I was instantly hooked.

OPPOSITE: Eggs in an egg: a twist on the traditional chopped egg garnish. The mild tasting, creamy-textured egg complements the sharp tang of the salty caviar. ABOVE: The best foil for caviar, a bubbly glass of Champagne serves as a refreshing palate cleanser.

No, that happened later, somewhere along the journey to adulthood, when I did acquire a taste both for those shining, dark fish eggs and for the sparkling libation that seemed inevitably to go with them. Over the years, this taste gradually turned into a hankering, then finally into a deep, intense craving that I satisfy as often as my budget allows. There is nothing more indulgent than a Champagne-and-caviar service, whether you are entertaining several of your closest friends, or are in the mood to treat yourself, by yourself.

I have developed my own personal ritual for serving Champagne and caviar, which involves a pile of warm cornmeal blinis (see page 97 for the recipe)

flutes of an austere, bone-dry bubbly. The eggs are presented in their tin or jar, which is set into a shallow saucer filled with crushed ice. Each guest is invited to pile the eggs high onto a blini, using the requisite mother-of-pearl spoon that was a Christmas present from a caviar-loving confederate.

Some people eat the whole blini in one mouthful, garnished with the lemon juice, melted butter, and crème fraîche I keep at the ready in cut crystal bowls. I prefer mine neat, as it were, and in nibbles, just small tastes of blini and roe, nothing to distract my mouth from the creamy eggs that explode with a sweet, saline flavor as I press my tongue to the roof of my mouth. Then, a sip of Champagne, whose tiny bursting bubbles mimic the sensation of the eggs,

and another bite of bliss-topped blini. There are few food experiences as sublime. In the pages that follow, I invite you to discover the magic of caviar and Champagne—each uniquely delightful... but irresistible in combination.

ABOVE: The perfect caviar spoon is an essential part of any service. Spoons of bone, mother-of pearl, and horn epitomize elegance. Stainless steel or plastic will do, but never use silver, which will both tarnish and affect the taste of the caviar. **OPPOSITE**: A silver *presentoir* with three bowls means you can offer your guests a selection of several different types of caviar and/or other roe.

Precious Eggs

The world's most seductive treasures can often be found stashed within ugly confines. Just as a gnarled, barnacled oyster can be opened to reveal a pale, luminous pearl, or a mangy mutt might possess the most loyal and friendly of canine dispositions, so does the bloated, rough-skinned sturgeon hold the precious cargo that is caviar. True caviar is made from the roe (eggs) of the sturgeon.

To the caviar connoisseur, the finest caviar comes
from the sturgeon of the Caspian Sea.

Sturgeon (genus *Ascipenser)* belong to an ancient species that remains largely unchanged from its 100 million-year-old ancestors. While fish are generally classified under two broad headings, those with bony skeletons and those with cartilaginous structures, the sturgeon falls into its own special category because it is both. The head is covered with scutes (bony plates), and five rows of these plates run the length of the fish's body. The plates are important because they add a hard structure to the fish, whose spine is cartilaginous. Sturgeon vary in color, but are generally white or grey with blue, black, grey, and/or greenish markings along the back, depending upon the type. Sturgeon are toothless creatures. In saline waters,

sturgeon feed on plankton. In fresh waters they use four sensitive tactile barbels on the underside of the snout to search the river bottom for small invertebrates such as worms, insect larvae, crayfish, mollusks, small fishes and plant life.

Scientists have identified twenty-three species of sturgeon, all native to the temperate waters of the Northern Hemisphere. While there are some solely freshwater species, most sturgeon make their home in the sea and swim upriver to spawn. This is the only time the fish produce the roe we prize as caviar. Unfortunately for caviar lovers, the sturgeon is stingy in her spawning habits, and does so only once every few years, in spring or summer. Not all sturgeon species produce roe that is harvested for caviar, but those that do may yield 10 to 20 percent of their body weight in eggs.

The sturgeon eggs (and the caviar made from them) can vary greatly in color. In fact, an individual fish may produce several different colors of roe,

OPPOSITE: Salmon roe, with its gorgeous intensity of color, can brighten up the typically monochromatic caviar service of belugas, osetras, and sevrugas.

depending on the weather. The natural pigmentation of a particular fish will also affect the color of its eggs. And, when the female is caught closer to spawning (releasing the eggs), those more mature eggs are lighter in color; immature eggs are darker and may even appear black.

Most sturgeon are found in the seas and rivers of Eastern Europe and in North American freshwaters, although there is also a substantial population in China. To the caviar connoisseur, the finest caviar, to which no other roe can compare, comes from the sturgeon of the Caspian Sea. Part of the reason for this situation is that the Caspian Sea is landlocked and therefore unaffected by currents. This body of water also has the salinity and type of plankton that are believed to create the perfect living conditions for sturgeon. Finally, one can assume that the caviar processors in this region, with their centuries of experience and proud traditions, help to make the final product something special.

OPPOSITE: A delightful alternative to the traditional blini is a crêpe topped with caviar and accompanied by a dollop of crème fraîche or sour cream—and, of course, a tall flute of Champagne.

A Word on Salmon Roe

Well into the 19th century, salmon were plentiful throughout Western Europe and North America; indeed, salmon was considered a common poor-man's food in many places. Now, as with sturgeon fishing, salmon catches are regulated by the US and Canadian governments, and conservation measures are in place.

Alaska is one of the biggest producers of salmon caviar, most of which, until recently, was exported to Japan, where it is considered a great delicacy. The Japanese call it ikura. *Today salmon caviar has found its place in the North American market, and most suppliers of caviar also stock salmon roe.*

Although it cannot bear the prestigious designation of "caviar" on its label, salmon roe is well worth trying. The roe, which range in hue from golden orange to orange-red, are bigger than beluga caviar and have a tangier, more lively flavor than sturgeon roe. Salmon caviar is best enjoyed spread on toast or a blini, or used to garnish delicate hors d'oeuvres.

Types of Caviar

Caviar is named according to the type of sturgeon that it comes from. Beluga, osetra and sevruga are the three most common types.

Beluga
Huso huso or Acipenser hugo

The beluga sturgeon is found in the Caspian Sea, the Black Sea, and the Sea of Azov. It is the largest of sturgeon, and can grow to 15 feet (4.5m) long and weigh up to 2,500 pounds (1,125kg), though most weigh between 800 and 900 pounds (360-405kg). It is a

monstrous-looking fish with a bony-plated back and a long snout. Belugas have a life span of one hundred years, but the female does not reach breeding (that is, caviar-producing) age until she is twenty. A beluga may contain up to 130 pounds (59kg) of eggs. The roe, which ranges in color from deep steely grey to a variegated white, is the biggest of all types of sturgeon roe (about 2½ to 3 millimeters in diameter), and therefore the most expensive (size definitely matters in caviar economics). And beluga roe do deliver a most satisfying pop against the roof of the mouth. Many people, however, prefer the slightly sweeter flavor of the osetra.

Osetra
Acipenser gueldenstaedtii

Found only in the Caspian Sea, this sturgeon has a long snout like the beluga, but grows only to six feet (2m) in length, weighing from 200 to 550 pounds (90-248kg). The female can begin producing roe at twelve to fourteen years instead of twenty. The osetra sturgeon produces the next-largest eggs after the beluga, and the eggs vary in color from golden-brown to greenish or grey. Many people consider osetra, with its mellow, almost fruity flavor, the finest tasting caviar of all.

There are twenty-three species of sturgeon,
but not all of them produce caviar.

In the early twentieth century, caviar was served free in American bars, like pretzels.

Sevruga

Acipenser stellatus

Sevrugas, like osetras, are found only in the Caspian Sea. The smallest of the three, the sevruga grows to between 50 and 100 pounds (22-40kg) at its full 4-foot (1.2m) length. Of the three most common sturgeon, it is the most distinctive looking, with an unusual scythe-shaped snout. The female matures quite young for sturgeon, at only seven years. Sevrugas are the most abundant species of sturgeon and produce the smallest (and least expensive) eggs. The roe, which can range in color from dark gray to black, is the most reliably consistent in flavor, and has a more pronounced saline character than the other two varieties. The eggs of the sevruga are quite small and have a rather soft texture, which is not conducive to oral bursting. Sevruga is, nevertheless, a delicious indulgence.

OPPOSITE: Caviar can transform the most humble appetizer into an unforgettable hors d'oeuvre, like this pastry pouch cleverly garnished with just a smidgen of roe—enough to make it a memorable morsel.

Keluga

Huso dauricus

A close relative of the beluga, this huge fish comes from the Amur and other rivers located in northern Manchuria, where it can grow to be 2,000 pounds (900kg) and yield as much as 400 pounds (180kg) of precious dark eggs. The caviar is marketed under the name keluga, and is of excellent quality, with medium-size berries, a deep black color, and excellent salinity. Keluga also provides a delightful pop in the mouth. The price is just as high as that of the Russian roe.

Golden Caviar

Shimmering beads of the palest "golden caviar" are considered a rare delicacy. Not to be confused with the more intensely yellow caviar that comes from the sterlet (the smallest species of sturgeon), golden caviar comes only from albino sturgeon of any of the above species. Golden caviar is reputedly so seductive in flavor that it was once reserved exclusively for the tsars; today almost the entire harvest of this rare delicacy remains within Russia and Iran to be enjoyed by the native elite.

A female sturgeon may be heavy with eggs; indeed, sturgeon eggs can comprise up to 20 percent of the fish's total weight.

A Roe By Any Other Name...

In France and other European countries, in order to be labeled as caviar, fish roe must come from a sturgeon. The Unites States and Canada are a bit more lax in their designations, and allow any type of seafood roe to be called caviar as long as the label specifies the type of creature the roe came from, such as "salmon caviar," "golden whitefish caviar," and "lumpfish caviar." Only sturgeon caviar can be called just plain "caviar." These other roes are wonderful to serve along with caviar for a glorious and diverse tasting. They also pad the offerings, making it easier to serve less of the expensive, genuine caviar.

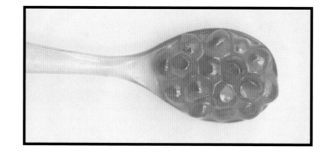

Salmon Caviar

Vermillion orbs of salmon caviar are probably my favorite of all non-sturgeon roe. The eggs are not graded, and this makes for easier processing, which is reflected in the relatively reasonable price. Salmon caviar may range in hue from golden to deep amber to bright orangey-red. The eggs are quite large and make a juicy pop. The taste is more intense and saltier than that of sturgeon caviar, and the texture is somewhat oilier.

Lumpfish Caviar

Favored by caterers and popularly used in the infamous three-layer caviar pie, lumpfish caviar is inexpensive enough to be served regularly. The originally transparent eggs are heavily salted and then flamboyantly dyed (with cuttlefish ink or vegetable dyes) either red, gold, or black, purely for aesthetic reasons. Lumpfish roe is not highly esteemed, but it does improve with a good rinsing, and can make a tasty enough garnish for a salmon mousse if salmon roe is not available. It can also be used in dip recipes, where its salty flavor is mitigated.

Golden Whitefish Caviar

Glistening golden-yellow whitefish caviar is gaining popularity across North America. Whitefish, from the Great Lakes region, produce tiny eggs that have a pleasantly mild flavor and a delightful crunch. They make an especially striking garnish and, because of their small size and low oil content, are the only caviar that can be stored in the freezer without turning to mush!

Other Seafood Roe

Although the sturgeon is a one-of-a-kind fish, it does have relatives, such as the paddlefish (also called the duckbill cat), a freshwater species with a paddle-like snout, wide mouth, smooth skin, and cartilaginous skeleton. The roe of this fish can be made into something similar to, if not nearly as sublime as, true caviar.

Rarely called caviar, pinkish-hued cod roe is easy to procure and very savory. Often sold pressed (since the eggs are almost microscopically tiny), the roe can be wrapped in cheesecloth and simmered until firm, then sliced and fried. The smoked roe is also popular and can be eaten as is.

Similar to cod eggs in their tiny size, carp and mullet roes are ubiquitous in Mediterranean countries and in Eastern Europe. In Greece, they are called tarama, and made into a dip called taramasalata. Tarama has a long shelf life, and a tightly resealed jar may be stored for several weeks in the refrigerator. The roes of flying fish (saline and brisk), crab (bittersweet and crunchy), cod (fishy and pasty), herring (also called shad; crisp and salty) and sea urchin (creamy and pungent) are processed and used in sushi in Japan and sometimes in the West. Wasabi caviar is actually flying fish roe that has been flavored and colored with fiery powdered wasabi (a type of radish, which is colored green in powdered form).

The Word Caviar

The linguistic history of caviar takes us all the way to Turkey. The Turkish khavyar became caviale in Italian, cabial in Spanish, cavial in French, and caviar in Portuguese. In the late sixteenth century, when caviar was first introduced to the Western world, it went by a rather motley collection of spellings, including "chauile," "cavery," and "cauiarie." Until about 1625, when the final "e" was dropped, "caviare" was pronounced in the Italian style, with four syllables. According to Jonathan Swift, the eighteenth-century fashion was to pronounce it in just two syllables, "caveer" (to rhyme, of course, with cheer). Our modern, tri-syllabic pronunciation has no doubt been influenced by the French. So, although Russia has given us this great delicacy, and popularized terminologies such as beluga, osetra, and sevruga, we have made a conscious decision, after a brief trial period, not to adopt the rather homely Russian name for sturgeon roe, ikra.

Caviar History

Caviar has been considered many things by many people. It has been prized by the elite throughout history, but for everyman, caviar was not always considered the delicacy that it is today.

Caviar, as it appears in written history, dates back to the eighth century B.C.E., when the ancient Greeks ate it pickled and salted. In the fourth century B.C.E., Aristotle's crowd evidently enjoyed caviar at many a feast. Sturgeon was considered the finest fish in the world at the time of the mighty Roman Empire, and the caviar was given a suitably regal presentation at the table, where it was placed on a bed of flowers to the chorus of trumpets and flutes. We know that the Chinese were processing and trading caviar during the tenth century (after first simmering the roe in an infusion of acacialike seeds, then pickling it in brine). And generations of Russian tsars have enjoyed the luxury of caviar.

OPPOSITE: For an epicurean adventure, host a caviar tasting party: offer your guests a choice and enjoy the contrasts among the different colors, sizes, textures, and tastes of the various roe.

In twelfth-century Britain, Henry II declared the sturgeon a "royal fish" that, when caught, had to be forfeited to the kitchens of the feudal lords. Four centuries later, caviar was becoming increasingly well known, since abundant supplies of sturgeon made it the cheapest fish in southern France, where it inhabited the estuary of the Rhône. Even so, the roe was not much appreciated, except by the wealthy. Rabelais wrote of "caviat" in *Pantagruel* and Shakespeare used caviar as a metaphor in *Hamlet*. Pope Julius II praised it in 1520, by which time sturgeon and caviar had become established as favorite delicacies among the royalty and aristocracy of Europe.

Outside Russia and the formal dining rooms of the European elite, caviar really became popular when two brothers, known as Melkon and Mougcheg, traveled from their Russian homeland to Paris, France. When they left, the Tsar was still in power, but while they were in Paris, in 1917, the People's Revolution took place and the Tsar was overthrown. Stunned to find caviar missing entirely from the Parisian diet, the brothers inquired to Russia about importing some. At first they were told that Russia had nothing to sell abroad, but then the officials realized that millions of hungry Russians could not survive on caviar alone, and that if they exported it, they would gain valuable hard currency with which to buy wheat. Russian caviar arrived in Paris in 1920 and immediately appealed to the richer segment of Parisians because of its high price tag. But marketing the product to a broader consumer base proved somewhat difficult.

At the Gastronomic Exhibition in Paris, the Russian brothers, who had by then acquired the primary importing rights on caviar, had to install spittoons around their tasting booths, since most people had a rather nasty first impression of the stuff. Those with "good taste," however, approved and, as their taste influenced the crowd, caviar eventually became popular.

In fact, for much of history, the middle and lower classes showed a general indifference toward caviar, and sturgeon eggs were simply eaten as a normal part of the diet, along with the rest of the fish. For a long time, the only westerners who ate caviar regularly were poor fishermen, who had to remove the undesirable eggs before they could sell the sturgeon they had caught. Native Americans who lived along the Pacific and Atlantic coasts made both sturgeon and salmon, and their nutritious roe, mainstays of their diet, eating them plain, pickling them, or making them into a smoked, cheeselike preparation. American saloons and

OPPOSITE: Simple yet divine: sturgeon caviar and salmon roe garnish smoked salmon-topped blinis in these charming hors d'oeuvres.

In the early twentieth century, caviar was served free in American bars, like pretzels.

bars actually provided salty caviar for free (along with oysters and clams), to build a thirst for beer. Indeed, Americans did not prize the delicate little roe until the turn of the nineteenth century.

Then, over the course of about twenty years, from around 1880 to 1900, North American caviar businesses began to take off at an astonishing rate, exporting tons of caviar to Europe each year. Russian caviar was being touted as the finest quality caviar, so some North American producers shipped much of their supply to Europe, where they had it repackaged and shipped back as "Russian caviar."

In 1900 sturgeon were still being caught in the Hudson River and other rivers that drain into the Atlantic and Pacific oceans. Sturgeon were also fished in France from the Seine, and in the southern part of

LEFT: What could be more romantic than caviar on ice and a bottle of the best Champagne? Consider making it a picnic...

the North Sea, the Baltic, the Black Sea, the Sea of Azov, and the Caspian Sea. But caviar's popularity soon sent these populations into decline.

The belief in a seeming endless supply of sturgeon was mistaken—the sturgeon population could not stand up to the sudden explosion of overfishing, and the supply of fish, which take years to reproduce, was quickly exhausted. By the turn of the twentieth century, the American fishing industry noticed a marked decline in numbers of sturgeon caught. Legislation was passed that regulated the fishing of sturgeon and banned fishermen from catching or harming immature sturgeon. Nevertheless, overfishing has remained a problem, and pollution has also taken a toll.

With the decline of the American sturgeon came a drastic rise in prices and a need to import caviar from Russia and Iran. To meet consumer demand, marketing savvy called for the introduction of other types of "caviar," including the delightful red roe of salmon, grey lumpfish roe and, in 1982, roe from the whitefish, whose golden eggs are beautiful and mild in flavor.

OPPOSITE: A traditionally Russian combination in a clever, modern presentation: this silver and crystal presentoir ices the caviar and vodka simultaneously.

From Ocean to Table: Harvesting and Processing Caviar

Fish roe, which is rather bland, does not become caviar until it has been processed with salt. But first, it needs to be harvested, or removed from the female sturgeon. The fishing, which is conducted with nets in the estuaries of the Caspian, is generally done once in the spring and once in the fall, during spawning season, as the fish return to fresh waters. Each fishing season lasts four months. The conditions of the river bottom will affect the taste of the fish and caviar. The more churned up the bottom (from heavy rains, for example), the muddier-tasting the caviar. Apart from the highly valued roe of the female sturgeon, males are appreciated for their flesh and spinal marrow, vesiga, a gelatinous substance that is used to make *coulibiac*, a prized multi-layered fish pastry. Isinglass is a form of gelatin that comes from the fish's air bladders. Rarely used today, in the past it was used widely to clarify wine and to make glues and jellies.

The extraction of the female's eggs must be done with speed and precision. Thirteen fish can be processed in about fifteen minutes. Live female sturgeon are brought to the operating room–like processing center, where first they are struck on the head to knock them out. Each fish is weighed and tagged, and a long incision is made on the belly. The roe sacs are removed, opened, and placed on a huge sieve with holes just slightly larger than the eggs. The sacs are slowly rolled over the sieve and the eggs are caught in a stainless steel bucket below.

The operation is performed while the fish is alive because the egg membranes in a dead fish deteriorate so rapidly that they would rupture. In California, experimental caesarian sections were performed on sturgeon to allow their release afterwards, so they would produce more roe. The procedure was not successful, however, as it was discovered that when the fish underwent stress, they secreted adrenaline, which softened the eggs and made them unmarketable. Research on other preservationist methods of roe collection is currently underway.

The harvested eggs are rinsed in fresh water and drained before the caviar master takes over. The master must examine and taste the roe and make a quick decision to determine its grade. He looks for a uniform grain consistency in the mouth, as well as size, color, gleam, firmness, and the vulnerability of the roe skin. The largest and lightest-colored eggs are the rarest, and thus become the most expensive caviar.

Then the master determines how much salt to add. Salt both preserves the roe and heightens its flavor. It is desirable to use as little salt as possible, but the roe must be top quality and of uniform size and color to receive this treatment. Caviar that contains added salt of less than five percent of the total weight of the roe is labeled malossol, "little salt," and is the most flavorful and highly desirable. (Be wary, though—there are no laws in the United States and Canada to enforce this percentage or to regulate labeling that specifies "malossol.") All of these evaluations must be made within two or three minutes since unsalted roe deteriorates quite quickly.

OPPOSITE: In the 12th century, King Henry II of England decreed sturgeon the "royal fish." During his reign, all caviar was reserved exclusively for the pleasure of members of the royal elite.

The salt used to treat the roe once came exclusively from deposits in the Astrakhan Steppe in Russia, but after 1941 chlorine was added to the water there and that source was no longer pure. Today, a chemically purified salt is used. Borax is often used in addition to salt, since it helps preserve the roe, which consequently needs less salt. The result is a sweeter flavor and less skin shrinkage in the caviar. Very large amounts of borax are toxic, however, and use of the substance in caviar processing is banned by the United States Food and Drug Administration, so borax-treated caviar is not imported into the United States. Borax is used for caviar destined for elsewhere, however, and borated caviar is much preferred in many parts of Europe.

The salt, or salt and borax mixture, is mixed with the roe by hand. A brine forms, as much of the fat is drawn off by the salt. The roe is placed on fine-mesh sieves and gently tossed until it dries. Now the roe is considered caviar, and is transferred into two-kilo tins, whose lids are varnished so the caviar does not become tainted with a metallic nuance. The tins are labeled and sealed airtight. They are then shipped in refrigerated or iced containers.

OPPOSITE: Golden caviar is a rare treat, once reserved for the exclusive consumption of the Tsar.

Fresh malossol caviar, which is considered the very finest and most expensive of all caviars, must be brought quickly to market and sold within weeks. Pasteurized malossol (caviar that has been packed into small jars, hermetically vacuum-sealed, and partially cooked) can be stored for about a year at room temperature. The taste, texture, and consistency of pasteurized caviar do suffer, but it is less expensive than fresh caviar, and still considered delicious.

"Barrel" caviar is different from malossol caviar only in that more salt is used in the processing. In March and early April, the beginning of the spring catch, most roe is firm and can be made into malossol caviar. By late April and early May the increase in temperature means that the roe becomes less firm. As a result, late-season roe is usually made into barrel or pressed caviar.

Pressed caviar is made from very mature, late-season roe and broken or otherwise damaged eggs. The cleaned, salted eggs are placed in a linen or cheesecloth sack and squeezed in a machine. About 20 percent of the fatty liquid is pressed out during this process; the egg mass is then packed into two-kilo tins and shipped. It takes about five pounds (2.3kg) of fresh roe to make one pound (.45kg) of pressed caviar. Pressed caviar has a jamlike texture and very intense taste that is revered by many connoisseurs. It is best served with blinis and sour cream.

A Shrinking Supply

Gone are the days when sturgeon filled the seas and caviar was harvested by the ton. In the late 1800s America produced the second largest amount of caviar after Russia. Now, about 90 percent of America's caviar is imported from the countries around the Caspian Sea (except for Iran, whose products are banned), the only waters where sturgeon live in any quantity.

But the Caspian is no Eden, and increasing environmental hazards, compounded by rampant poaching, have taken a serious toll on the sturgeon population. This

ABOVE: Caviar must be kept icy cold; the presentoir, filled with crushed ice, does the job to perfection.

OPPOSITE: An assortment of caviar-garnished hors d'oeuvres can transform a cocktail party into an elegant soirée.

means that the caviar supply is shrinking, and will probably continue to shrink, causing caviar prices to rise to levels prohibitive to most people. Here is a look at the situation as it stands today.

You could say that one problem has arisen from nature's whimsy. The level of the Caspian dropped significantly early in the twentieth century, and has shrunk an astounding eight feet (2.4m) in the last thirty years. This phenomenon (due mostly to evaporation) has meant fewer spawning and feeding grounds for the sturgeon. Although the waters have been rising since 1978, and the sea is currently at the level it was at in 1930, sturgeon populations are not expected to recover significantly. No one knows exactly why the sea level changes, but if it continues to rise it may reach soils that have been contaminated with radioactive materials from the days of nuclear bomb testing—yet another lurking threat to the species of the Caspian.

Man-made problems include dams and hydroelectric power plants that have been built along the rivers that feed into the sea, preventing sturgeon from making their pilgrimage upstream in order to spawn. Oil, which yields greater profits than caviar, presents yet another hazard for the sturgeon who share their "turf"

with this other exploited natural resource. Agricultural runoff and industrial waste goes unchecked as it finds its resting place in the Caspian. Since the Caspian is tiny compared to other seas, it is more at risk of being overwhelmed with pollutants. All this extra pollution means a decrease in oxygen levels in the sea, and reduced ability of plankton, the sturgeon's main food source, to photosynthesize.

Although the Russian government has taken some proactive measures to aid the struggling sturgeon population, such as restocking the Caspian Sea with 50 million baby sturgeon each year, breeding and restocking is generally unrewarding with a species that has such a long life cycle. And widespread poaching, spurred on by the incredibly high prices caviar can bring on the New York or Paris market, mean that most of these fish end up on the wrong end of a fishing line before they even have the chance to mature and spawn.

OPPOSITE: Sometimes a simple, minimalist presentation can prove the most stunning. Here, two modern glass bowls in different sizes form an effective presentoir.

Caviar is extremely nutritious. It contains 47 vitamins and minerals, with only 74 calories per ounce.

There are anti-poaching squads organized by the Russian fisheries police, but they have proven little match for the poachers, who can make as much money in a single hour as the police make in an entire month. Mass unemployment and the collapse of the shipping industry in the Volga River delta have pushed many of the one million people of that region to turn to illegal fishing.

During the past ten years, sturgeon harvests have decreased by a dramatic 90 percent. The last recorded full-grown sturgeon was a sixty-year-old beluga weighing in at 2,163 pounds (973kg), including 265 pounds (119kg) of caviar, caught in 1989. The big fish is currently on display in a regional museum as a memory of the bountiful past. Sadly, it is possible that caviar will become a Proustian treat—one that can be enjoyed only in our memories—if the situation does not change drastically.

OPPOSITE: The largest roe come from the beluga sturgeon, and produce an intense burst of flavor when popped against the roof of the mouth.

Buying and Storing Caviar

Choosing which kind is one of the hardest things about buying caviar. While in general I can say that osetra has been my favorite (I like the rounded, soft flavor of the eggs, and their compelling burst of salt when they open onto my tongue), I have also had superior sevrugas and exceptional, worth-the-price belugas, too. Often a serious gourmet shop will let you taste a bit of the caviar before buying, while the bargain places tend to be less accommodating. In any case the important thing is to go to a place known for its caviar. This will ensure a high turnover, and the freshest product.

If you want to serve the best of the best, buy only malossol caviar—fresh caviar processed with the smallest amount of salt. Look for eggs that glisten attractively, and that are plump and moist, but not oily. Most books tell you that it is polite to serve from one to two ounces (28-56g) of caviar per person. I'll tell you that you can get away with less if you round out the offerings with blinis or boiled little red potatoes cut in half

Fresh caviar is extremely perishable and must be kept cool. The roe should have a fresh, briny smell and be firm, shiny and not clumped together.

to spread with the caviar, a platter of smoked fish, and plenty of Champagne or iced Russian vodka. But the minimum you should have is half an ounce (14g) per person, and if that seems too hard on the wallet, consider adding other types of less expensive fish roe to the service such as those from salmon, whitefish, lumpfish, trout, crab, or flying fish.

Once you buy your caviar, go straight home, unless you have brought along an ice pack and an insulated bag (and even then it doesn't pay to dawdle). Fresh (unpasteurized) caviar can be stored for several days, even up to a few weeks, unopened in the refrigerator. The best way to keep it is to place the tin in a resealable plastic bag, then place it in a larger resealable plastic bag filled with ice. Place the bundle in the coldest part of your refrigerator and remove only just before serving time.

After the caviar has been opened it is best eaten immediately, and it must be consumed within a day or two. Leftover caviar is rarely a problem, though, and if you should find yourself with a bit, enjoy your bounty as soon as possible. You needn't worry about detecting whether your caviar has gone off—the forbidding scent will tell you as soon as your open the jar!

For those times when caviar is desired, but fresh caviar is unaffordable or inappropriate, pasteurized caviar is also a treat. Since the roe is cooked, however, something essential is sacrificed, and connoisseurs feel that fresh salmon or even lumpfish caviar is often preferable to pasteurized beluga. The choice also depends on the brand. Pasteurized caviar will last for several months unopened at room temperature, but after the seal is broken it, too, must be eaten within a few days, three at most. While some pasteurized sturgeon caviars are good enough to serve with all the pomp and circumstance of the fresh, other types (such as pasteurized lumpfish caviar) are better served as garnishes or stirred into cooked dishes (at the last moment, so as to barely heat the eggs).

It is difficult to give a guide for the quantity of pasteurized caviar to serve, but a rough estimate might be two ounces per person for eating straight, and less for garnishing.

OPPOSITE: Salmon caviar is less expensive than sturgeon caviar, but it is delicious all the same. The large bright orange or red roe are very full-flavored.

The Perfect Presentation

There is no single right way to serve caviar, but there is one serious mistake that will severely curtail one's enjoyment of the pristine eggs. Never, ever serve caviar straight at room temperature. If the caviar is meant to stand on its own (that is, it will not be mixed into a dip or other such preparation), it must be served as close to ice cold as it can get without freezing (which would turn it to soup).

That said, there are myriad ways to enjoy the minuscule fish egg, the most important being the way you like it best. But there is more to presentation than the actual eggs. There is the ambience of the whole evening to consider, down to the tablecloth, centerpiece, music, and lighting. This may sound pretentious, but since you have decided to serve a delicacy (and have spent a lot of money on a few small tins of fish roe), why not make the most of it? The ceremony seems both justified and appropriate. So set the table as

OPPOSITE: The petite sevruga produce the smallest caviar of all the sturgeon. Their roe range in color from dark grey to black, and have a distinct saline flavor.

Pointers for the Perfect Service

- *A presentoir is a decorative serving bowl, usually consisting of a small glass or crystal dish that nests inside a larger silver or crystal bowl filled with crushed ice*
- *If you don't have a presentoir or would prefer a more casual service, leave the caviar in its open tin and place it in a shallow bowl of crushed ice*
- *Minced onion, chopped egg, lemon wedges, crème fraîche, sour cream, and capers all make interesting and tasty garnishes*
- *Keeping the eggs nice and cool at all times is key; make sure that the plates your guests will be eating from have been chilled in advance*
- *A small decorative serving spoon and a gentle hand insures that the delicate eggs will remain intact right up to the moment they are consumed*
- *Do not allow any silver to come in contact with the roe*
- *Select a dry Champagne for the most inspired pairing with caviar*
- *If you are serving vodka, chill it in the freezer well beforehand. The vodka will not freeze due to its high alcohol content; rather it will become deliciously smooth and syrupy. Keep the bottle of vodka in a bucket of crushed ice*

grandly as your stock of table dressings allows. Now is the time for the finest linen table cloths, the most translucent bone china, and the loveliest crystal glasses. The only fancy tableware not to use is silver, since it can give the caviar a metallic taste, and the caviar can discolor your spoon. Instead, if you have them, use your mother-of-pearl, horn, or bone caviar spoons. Barring that, stainless steel and even plastic will do.

Then, decide how you want to serve the eggs. Are you in the mood for a purist treat, and want nothing to diminish the pleasure of pure caviar? Then you must first make sure that your caviar is up to snuff. Buy the freshest malossol caviar your pocketbook allows. It

doesn't matter which type you choose, as long as it is fresh and glossy, with firm shining beads. Beluga certainly has the most status, but osetra is a favorite among those in the know, and sevruga is good for a crowd. If

ABOVE: The actress Brigitte Bardot once declared: "Champagne is the one thing that gives me zest when I feel tired." **OPPOSITE:** Pressed caviar is made from a combination of different roe that have been damaged or are especially fragile. Spread it on toast or blini for an unforgettable treat.

you have a caviar *presentoir* (a special caviar server that consists of a glass or crystal bowl that fits snugly inside a larger silver bowl to be filled with ice shavings), use it here. Otherwise, you can improvise a presentoir. Carefully spoon the caviar into the center bowl and set the presentoir on the table only when all the guests have arrived. Let them heap some of the caviar onto cold plates, to be enjoyed as it is, with a spoon.

If you feel that you need a more elaborate caviar service, by all means, garnish. As long as the garnishes are served on the side, you won't displease those who cannot bear to see their caviar adulterated in any way. But for others, garnishes can enhance the overall experience of caviar eating. Blinis, freshly buttered toast points, or even crisp melba toasts are standard fare, but never serve crackers, since their brittle texture interferes with the bursting caviar eggs. You can either buy or make the blinis, but if you decide to serve toast, make it yourself from soft, fresh bread, and always cut the crusts off. Butter the toast or not, depending on your taste.

Other suitable garnishes, which can be served in little bowls surrounding the caviar, include melted butter, chopped hard-boiled egg (serve the whites and yolks sep-

OPPOSITE: A solid block of ice makes a simple and very elegant service for caviar and its vodka accompaniment.

arately), minced onion, and lemon wedges. Crème fraîche and sour cream are also nice, although most people take them only with the more intense pressed caviar. Again, there is no right way to eat caviar. After what you have paid for it, you are entitled to eat it exactly as you please.

A Word About Vodka

Serving caviar with vodka instead of Champagne is a very traditional Russian way to enjoy the eggs. The clear, potent alcohol cleanses the palate between salty bites. For the most pleasing drink, freeze the vodka for several hours before serving it. This gives it a syrupy texture that caresses the tongue before sliding coolly down the gullet. If you have slim cylindrical glasses, use them for the vodka. If not, regular rocks glasses will do. Some people swear by drinking flavored vodka, such as lemon or orange, with their caviar. That is a nice variation, but stay away from hot pepper vodka, which can numb the palate and diminish your enjoyment of the caviar.

Pure Effervescence

Call it nectar of the gods, call it the culmination of human genius, call it the most marvelous wine that ever flowed from a glass bottle—there is no one way to define Champagne. Tangibly, it is an elegant, effervescent wine with a delicate color ranging from deepest ivory to a soft, salmon pink. In flavor, it can range from candy sweet and fruity to crisp, dry, and bracing. But this definition describes almost any kind of sparkling wine; a true Champagne is something much more specific.

In France, "le Champagne" is the wine and "la Champagne" is the region.

What is Champagne?

The term "sparkling wine" refers to all wine with carbon dioxide bubbles in it. Champagne, in the strictest sense, refers only to sparkling wine produced within the Champagne region of France—the country's northernmost wine-producing region, located about 90 miles (144km) east of Paris.

French winemaking standards are set by laws setting strict requirements for each wine-producing area. Known as the Appellation d'Origine Contrôlée laws, they were developed during the 1930s to regulate the wine making process, and cover geographic boundaries, grape varieties, minimum alcohol content, and vineyard methods. In the Champagne region, wines labeled Champagne must be made exclusively from Chardonnay (white), Pinot Meunier, or Pinot Noir (both red-skinned) grape varieties. These grapes must be processed only by the laborious, age-old Méthode Champenoise.

If, in Europe, a sparkling wine does not live up to these conditions, it may not be labeled Champagne, and instead terms such as sparkling wine or *vin mousseux* are used. In North America, any sparkling wine can carry a "champagne" (note the lowercase "c") label; the only restriction is that the carbonation must occur naturally (that is, carbon dioxide cannot be pumped in).

There are notable sparkling wines; lately some of them have given Champagne a run for its money. Nevertheless, true Champagne exists on a plane of its own and is a joy to imbibe.

OPPOSITE: Champagne should always be sipped from a Champagne flute. The tall, cylindrical design of the glass insures that the wine's bubbles are preserved.

Making Champagne

The Harvest

Accomplished entirely by hand, the harvest in *la Champagne* requires the help of 50–60,000 workers and lasts for about ten days in each village. It is the climax of the viticultural year and is always accompanied by a rush of excitement. The annual harvest is what drives all the worry, care, and attention throughout the growing season: careful train-ing, pruning, and trimming of the vines, protection against early winter and spring frosts, and the pervasive fear of potentially harmful weather conditions.

As soon as picking begins, the clusters of Pinot Noir, Meunier, and Chardonnay grapes are carefully selected and brought to the two thousand pressing houses scattered throughout the 312 villages in the Champagne region. But not until the juice is pressed,

ABOVE: Workers must pick thousands of bushels of grapes each year at the annual harvest in the Champagne region in Northeast France.

vinified, and racked will the Champenois relax. If the grapes are of the very best quality throughout *la Champagne*, many producers will elect to make vintage-dated wines (see Types of Champagne, p.70). When the quality of the grapes is less homogenous, fewer producers bottle vintage Champagnes.

The Art of
Assemblage

All sparkling wine starts with still wine pressed and fermented from the grapes of the harvest. Among the many steps necessary to craft Champagne wines, *assemblage,* or blending, is one of the most important, and is what distinguishes the Champagnes of the different houses. The late winter and early spring months (January to April) are devoted to blending base wines produced from the grapes of the fall harvest. Blending involves deciding which grape varieties to combine and in what proportions, which vintages (harvest years) to combine, and which vineyards' wines to use. Non-vintage Champagne starts from a base wine, the *vin de cuvée*, which is usually a blend of several vintages; vintage Champagne must contain wine from only that harvest year.

For centuries it has been observed that certain wine villages, or *crus*, produce more effervescent wines, while others produce grapes with more fruitiness or

more bite. Because of its northern location and the various micro-climates found throughout the region, Champagne experiences annual variations in the maturity, acidity, and sugar content of grapes. These characteristics vary from year to year and from cru to cru, depending on weather conditions during the growing season. The specific natural geography and climate of the region, known as the *terroir*, and the vintners' quest to create the perfect harmony of sweetness, acidity and flavor, are two elements that go into composing an assemblage. Each of the 312 crus in

ABOVE: Grapes are transported to the presses in traditional woven baskets. Several of the prestigious houses, such as Mumm, still use traditional wooden presses to process some of their harvest.

la Champagne encompasses a mosaic of plots of vineyards, known as a *galipe*. There are more than 300,000 galipes in Champagne, divided among 19,000 owners. Faced with variable harvests, in quality and quantity, the Champenois figured out that they could protect themselves from nature's vagaries by setting aside reserves (*blocages*) from good harvests, made of a portion of the year's better wines. These reserve wines are then used to complement the wines of future years when the assemblage is blended together. By blending base wines made from Pinot Noir, Meunier, or Chardonnay grapes from several villages and vintages, a whole is created that is better than any of its parts: more harmonious and better balanced, with complex fruitiness and depth of flavor, delicacy, and zing.

The three different grape varieties lend different specific elements to the assemblage. Pinot Noir, a black grape with white juice (grown mainly on the slopes of the mountain of Reims and in the Côte des Bar), gives aromas of berries to the wines, as well as body, complexity, and power. Pinot Meunier, another black grape (grown mainly in the Valley of the Marne), is supple and fruity with an intense, slightly spicy bouquet. Of the three, it matures fastest and rounds out the wine. Chardonnay, a white grape grown mainly in the Côte des Blancs, is a grape of delicacy and finesse. It gives floral and fruity aromas (and occasionally mineral overtones) when young, and it matures slowly, contributing to the complex development in the aging of Champagne wines.

To be successful at the art of assemblage, three qualities are necessary. These include an intimate knowledge of the vineyards, an understanding of the characters of the grapes from different sites and the ways in which they complement one another; an impeccable

ABOVE: The Champagne cork actually starts out as a cylinder, inserted partially into the neck of the bottle; over time it develops its familiar mushroom shape.

tasting memory based on the style of the house and the experience of several generations; and finally, creativity. Based on tasting after tasting, copious note-taking, a profound knowledge of wine, and in-depth testing, the irreversible assemblage takes place under the auspices of the well-educated blender. The blend should reflect the character and the traditions of the house or the grower who has created it.

method, and the bulk, or Charmat, process. In North America, manufacturers must indicate which method was followed on the label. On North American labels, the French method is stated as Méthode Champenoise or "Fermented in this bottle." The transfer process is indicated by "Fermented in the bottle." (Note the subtle difference in wording between the two, the latter indicating that the fermentation did not necessarily take place in the bottle the wine is being sold in.) Bulk sparking wines must state "Bulk" or "Charmat."

Methods of Refermentation

During the first fermentation, the sweet juice pressed from the grapes transforms into dry, still wine. The second fermentation (sometimes called refermentation) takes place in the bottles, where the added yeast consumes the residual sugars in the still wine, and the pressure of the resulting carbon dioxide is built up. It is this second fermentation that creates the bubbles and froth in sparkling wines.

There are three basic methods of refermentation, including the Méthode Champenoise, the transfer

Méthode Champenoise

It is this particular process of second fermentation that determines whether a sparkling wine meeting all the other requirements of the Appellation d'Origine

ABOVE AND OPPOSITE: Look for elegant and pleasing Champagne flute designs in delicate handblown glass or cut crystal.

It is rumored that Marilyn Monroe once took a bath
in 350 bottles of Champagne.

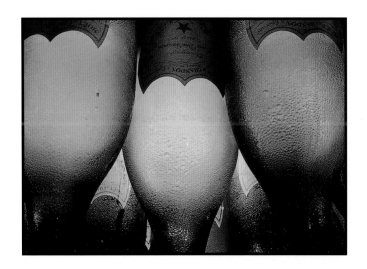

Contrôlée will be called Champagne. A solution of young wine, 17–24 grams of sugar, and yeasts, called the *liqueur de tirage*, is added to the vin de cuvée, or

OPPOSITE: A simple, beautifully shaped flute requires no ornamentation; simply fill it with the best bubbly and enjoy.

ABOVE: Bottles of Dom Pérignon undergoing the second fermentation in the bottle, where the characteristic bubbles will develop.

base wine, to induce the second fermentation. The bottle (the same one you will eventually see in the store) is sealed with a temporary cork or a metal crown cap and placed on its side to referment for three to four months, as the carbon dioxide builds and the yeast cells, or lees, flavor the wine. The wine must then stay "on the yeast" for at least one year, though some makers prefer to let their wines mature in this state for as long as five years.

Once the bubbles and flavors have formed, the dead yeast cells in the bottle must be removed by the process

The protruding part of the Champagne cork is known as the body and the part inside the bottle is called the wheel.

of *dégorgement* (disgorgement). To prepare for dégorgement the Champagne must first undergo the labor-intensive process of *remuage* (riddling). Every day for about six weeks, each bottle must be tilted and rotated slightly so that the sticky yeast sediment gradually becomes lodged in the neck of the bottle. Machinery has been developed to perform remuage, though hand turning is still performed by skilled *remueurs*. Mechanized gyropalettes are able to hold five hundred bottles each and twist them every eight hours, allowing remuage to be completed in just one week, as opposed to four weeks when performed by hand.

When the yeast sediment is settled in the neck of the bottle, the neck is immersed in a freezing brine solution that traps the sediment in a block of ice. The temporary cork is removed and the sediment block is expelled by the pressure of the carbon dioxide in the bottle. Since some liquid is lost during dégorgement,

LEFT: At certain houses, the process of *remuage* is still performed by hand. OPPOSITE: Viticulture has been one of the most economically important specialties of the Champagne region since the 15th century.

In 1993, 229 million bottles of Champagne were produced, 152.6 million bottles were shipped throughout France, and 76.4 million bottles were exported worldwide.

the house will usually add a mixture of sugar and some still wine of the same mixture as the Champagne, called *liqueur d'expedition.* The amount of sugar added is known as the dosage, and this determines the style, in terms of the sweetness level, of the resulting Champagne. Finally, a special multi-layered cork is inserted, a protective wire hood is attached, and the bottle is left to age so that the added dosage and the sparkling wine will blend.

Transfer Method

This method is much faster and less laborious than the Méthode Champenoise. Just as with the Méthode Champenoise, the vin de cuvée is bottled and the sugar-and-yeast solution is added to induce the second fermen-

RIGHT: A flute of light or medium-bodied Champagne is a delightful accompaniment to a first course.

tation. One difference is that after refermentation the sparkling wine is removed from the bottle and all of it is transferred to a huge pressurized tank, where it is filtered to remove the sediment and dead yeast cells, and then it is rebottled. This process is much cheaper than the Méthode Champenoise, but some of the character the wine develops during refermentation may be filtered out along with the sediment—although even wine experts sometimes have trouble distinguishing between a sparkling wine produced by the Méthode Champenoise and one made by the transfer method.

The Bulk or Charmat Process

This process was developed by Eugène Charmat, and is used to make the most inexpensive sparkling wines. The refermentation takes place in a large, closed tank rather than in individual corked bottles. After three or four weeks in the vat, the wine is filtered (as in the transfer method) and bottled. Bulk-process sparkling wines usually have undesirable large bubbles that tend to dissipate quickly in the glass, and wines produced in this way do not possess the traditional yeasty character of good Champagnes and sparkling wines.

OPPOSITE: A mimosa, also known as a "Buck's Fuzz," is a breakfast drink for a special occasion. It's made from one part orange juice to one part Champagne.

How Do You Like Your Champagne?

The strength of the final wine-and-sugar solution added to top off the bottle after dégorgement helps determine the sweetness of the Champagne, measured in grams per liter of residual sugar. An indication of sweetness appears on the label in the following terms:

Extra Brut, Brut Nature, *or* **Brut Sauvage** *The driest; contains 0–6 grams per liter of residual sugar.*

Brut *Dry; contains no more than 15 grams per liter of residual sugar.*

Extra Dry *Medium dry; contains 12–20 grams per liter of residual sugar.*

Sec *Slightly sweet; contains 17–35 grams per liter of residual sugar.*

Demi-Sec *Moderately sweet; contains 33–50 grams per liter of residual sugar.*

Doux *The sweetest; contains over 50 grams per liter of residual sugar (this style of Champagne is no longer produced).*

Types Of Champagne

Vintage Champagne

Traditionally, Champagnes are made by the assemblage of thirty to forty still wines, combining the products of different crus, grape varieties, and several different vintages—but vintage Champagne, as the name indicates, is made exclusively from grapes from a single year. Vintage Champagne comprises only about 20 percent of the Champagnes produced. For a vintage year to be designated, the harvest must have been a superb one, but vintage Champagne is not necessarily better than non-vintage (NV) Champagne. It should, however, be more distinctive and have a more definite character

The finest Champagne has the tiniest of bubbles. In fact, the French consider big bubbles so distasteful that they call them <u>l'oeil de crapaud</u> (toad's eyes).

than a non-vintage wine. Vintage Champagnes are also at least two years older than NV Champagnes. In a vintage year, the producers set aside a minimum of 20 percent of their crop as reserves to make still wines for present and future blending. Vintage Champagnes generally age for four to eight years on the lees before they are released to the trade, during which time they develop greater complexity and depth. Their remarkable balance is due to a perfect harmony between the sugar content, the acidity, and the aromatic characteristics of the grapes at harvest time. This balance changes every year, and only in an excellent year can it be showcased in vintage wines.

Like all Champagnes, vintage wines are ready to drink as soon as they are purchased, having been aged in the cellars of their producers prior to shipping.

OPPOSITE: A rare bottle of vintage Champagne—almost two centuries old! In general, newly released vintage Champagnes don't require more than six months' extra aging upon purchase.

However, they can also be kept for another five to ten years. In this case, they will develop an extra maturity, a nuttiness, and a roundness much appreciated by some wine lovers. One disadvantage is that older Champagnes and sparkling wines are apt to lose their bubbles quickly once they are opened and poured.

Special Champagnes

There are several special types of Champagne that are a cut above a regular bottle of bubbly. *Blanc de noirs* ("white of blacks") is made from the first pressing of black grapes (either Pinot Noir or Meunier) only, and may even be composed of 100 percent Pinot Noir. *Blanc de blancs* ("white of whites") is made from 100 percent Chardonnay grapes and tends to be lighter and more delicate than other Champagnes in its class.

Rosé Champagne is usually made from Pinot Noir and Chardonnay grapes exclusively and is processed by one of two methods. It may get its pink tint from the dark Pinot Noir skins as they steep in the vat—a method called maceration. Rosé may also be made by adding 10–15 percent still red wine—this is part of assemblage. Rosés are considered to be above average, and, like blanc de blancs, may be vintage or non-vintage. Since they are made with a greater proportion of black grapes than their light gold counterparts, rosé wines tend to be fruitier, although they can be just as dry. Often their aromas evoke strawberries, raspberries, and red and black currants. Like other brut Champagnes, rosés vary in style from one producer to another. Some will be light bodied and others fuller, in keeping with the producer's philosophy.

The French Ladder System

Champagne grape producing towns within the Champagne region are rated according to a quality control system called the *échelle des crus*, literally "ladder of growth." The Comité Interprofessionnel du Vin de Champagne (CIVC) is responsible for these rankings, which are based on vineyard factors that affect the quality of the grapes grown there, such as exposure to the sun and the other elements, drainage, and microclimate. Bottles labeled *grand cru* denote a Champagne made only with grapes from a village that has received a perfect 100 percent ranking on the *échelle des crus*. *Premier cru* signifies a village that has received a rating of 90–99 percent, and Champagne made exclusively with grapes from that village may be labeled as such. The remaining villages have ratings between 80 and 89 percent. Of the 312 villages in the region, only seventeen have *grand cru* ratings as of 1999.

LEFT: Connoisseurs savor the delicate pop of caviar followed by the pure effervescence of Champagne.

OPPOSITE: Bottles undergoing refermentation are housed in underground vaults where the temperature remains steady at around 45 to 50°F (7–10°C).

Although there is no set price for the harvested grapes, each year the growers and producers negotiate to define a benchmark price for that year. Prices are then distributed accordingly based on the percentage classification received by each village; for instance, grapes from a village classified at 88 percent can charge up to 88 percent of the top assigned price. On this basis, the grapes are sold to the Champagne houses.

What's in a Label?

Champagne classification does not stop with the name. There are a number of indications of style and production methods on the label, some required, others optional. The most important thing to look for is the guarantee that the wine is really Champagne. "Appellation of Controlled Origin" must be on the label. Another requirement, and one of the main indicators of style, is the inclusion of the house that produced the Champagne or sparkling wine,

which often appears at the top of the label. Perrier-Jouët, Veuve Clicquot Ponsardin, and Bollinger are examples, and different houses tend, overall, to produce wines of different degrees of lightness or richness.

Labels may be marked *Grand Marque* or *Tete de cuvée,* indicating that they are the finest of Champagnes. *Grand Marque* is the unofficial designation given in France to the best Champagne house. *Tete de cuvée* refers to the very best of the first juice to flow from the press (like an extra-virgin olive oil). *Cuvée* signifies the first 533 gallons (2,050l) of juice pressed from each 8,800lbs. (4000kg) of grapes. *Cuvée* on the label can indicate a finished blend which has been drawn from several different *cuvées.* The remain-ing portions of the pressing, *première taille* (the next 106 gallons [410l]) and *deuxième taille* (the final 54 gallons [206l]), are of a proportionately lesser quality and are used for the production of cheaper and usual-ly sweeter sparkling wines, though these words are not required to appear on the label. The degree of sweetness, such as brut, semi-brut, and so on, must appear on the label.

OPPOSITE: Close examination of the label on this vintage bottle of Moët et Chandon Dom Pérignon reveals the wine's provenance. **ABOVE:** The venerable Roederer is one of the finest Champagne houses.

Terms on the label such as *blanc de blancs* can indicate the grape variety used, and to some extent the resulting style of the wine, but they not required. On vintage Champagnes, the vintage is stated, indicating to experts, who have observed a certain house standard and the features of a certain year's harvest, what the wine might be like. Vintage wines must have a minimum alcohol content of 11 per cent, and indeed, a minimum alcohol content for Champagne is set each year in France, according to the specific qualities of that year's harvest. This alcohol content is usually close to 12 percent by volume, and is also listed on the label.

Along with the phrase, "Country of Origin: France," the village where the Champagne was made must be printed on the label. Since the village ratings rarely change, however, it is up to the Champagne lover to discover villages and producers that might be underrated. Finally, the importer is listed for sparkling wines imported to the United States and Canada.

OPPOSITE: "In victory you deserve it, in defeat you need it."—Napoleon

A Short History Lesson

Since time immemorial, the area of France now known as *la Champagne* has been producing wine of distinction. However, up until the seventeenth century, vintners worked at producing robust still wines with a cloudy salmon color and a syrupy flavor— nothing like the subtle, mostly dry, sparkling wines that are produced today. Wine-making was widespread. Around 1375 the Archbishop of Reims took an inventory showing that every village in the vicinity of Reims was employed in wine production. By 1412 the Reims charter, presented to Charles VI for his signature, claimed that viticulture had become the major source of economic activity in the town.

The geographical position of the Champagne region was such that it was vulnerable to attacks from invaders from the north attempting to reach the heart of France. However, its position as a gateway into the country also had its advantages. Champagne's villages turned into convenient centers for trade. Wine and cloth from the region was bartered for spices and other luxury goods from the south, which kept the towns prosperous and the wine makers ever striving to make better wine, which would be worth more in trade.

While most of Champagne's early wines were still, there were exceptions. Because of the way the climate of the region affected the fermentation (see below), some of the wines produced did have bubbles, but it was an unpredictable and often unwanted occurrence. It wasn't until the mid-seventeenth century that the process for producing Champagne as we know it (albeit a sweeter variety) was developed.

Dom Pérignon

The credit for the creation of true Champagne must be given to Dom Pérignon (1638–1715), a blind Benedictine monk and cellarmaster. Pérignon, christened Pierre, was noted for his above-average intellect and his scientific and methodical mind. Although blind at the time (he was twenty-nine), he was made steward of the monastery of Hautvillers near Epernay in Champagne, an estate that included 100 acres (40 hectares) of vineyards. Unlike many of his contemporaries, Pérignon enjoyed the bubbles that were sometimes found in bottles of the region's wines. Upon tasting a bottle of effervescent regional wine, Pérignon is said to have declared, "I am drinking stars." It became his life's work to capture those stars in every bottle of the wines of Champagne.

Demand for white wine was high and could only be met if the summer had been sunny enough to fully ripen the grapes. Pérignon developed a way to obtain

white wine from hardier black grapes by devising a method of pressing the grapes that allowed the juice to come into contact with the grape skins (which carry the yeast necessary for fermentation) for only just the right amount of time, but not long enough to color the juice red. His perfection of the art of pressing also led him to become the first to set aside the juice from the different stages of the pressing process. Apparently Dom Pérignon had a great memory, a

ABOVE: The famed father of Champagne, Benedictine monk Dom Pérignon.

superb sense of smell, and an exceptionally finely tuned palate, which enabled him to identify grape varieties and create superior blends.

Sparkling wines were discovered accidentally, and are simply the result of a refermentation of residual sugars and live yeast cells that remain following the wine's first fermentation. This occurred spontaneously in Champagne, depending on the weather. An early arrival of winter in the region meant that the natural process of fermentation would be put on hold as the temperature dropped and the wine partially froze (with some of the yeasts still present). In the spring, as the weather became warmer, the yeast cells awakened and fermentation began anew, releasing carbon dioxide into the wine and making it fizz. Refermentation also transforms a harsh, acidic wine made from barely ripe grapes into a more balanced and palatable sparkling wine due to the flavor imparted by the yeast.

Wine makers in cooler regions, where grapes tend not to ripen well, found this discovery invaluable. It was as early as 931 that medium-sweet, sparkling Blanquette de Limoux was accidentally produced and protected by a royal decree. But Dom Pérignon was the first to create a regulated wine from Champagne grapes that could be made intentionally and keep its effervescence.

Another wine-making monk, Frère Jean Oudart, from Chalons, began the use of *liqueur de tirage* as a way to purposely induce a second fermentation in the bottle.

It wasn't until he was sixty years old that Dom Pérignon produced a true Champagne as we know it today. Thanks to the cork—an invention that was "rediscovered" and brought to France from Spain (it had been around since Roman times)—and the development of thicker glass bottles (*verre anglais,* or English glass) that could withstand the high pressures of the carbon dioxide gas, Dom Pérignon's dream was realized.

Champagne A.D. (After Dom)

Dom Pérignon died in 1715 and was buried in his vineyard. The monastery at Hautvillers was destroyed during the French Revolution and there has never been a vine-growing monastery since. The first Champagne houses began to take over the monks' wine-making business during the eighteenth century. In 1794, the firm Moët et Chandon purchased the land and old vineyards of the monastery at Hautvillers and named their best wine Dom Pérignon. About ten other Champagne houses, including Ruinart (1729), Moët (1743), and Clicquot (1772), formed during the eighteenth century.

Although many of the older wine critics of the time scorned Champagne and deemed it frivolous, the exciting, effervescent libation drew a wealthy, trendsetting crowd to the newly established Champagne houses. French Regent Philippe

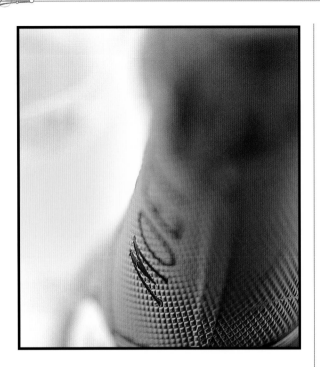

Mumm (1827), Bollinger (1829), Pommery (1836), Krug (1843), Pol Roger (1849), Mercier (1858) and Gratien (1864) all became established during this boom time, and these leading Champagne houses are still in existence today. By the mid-nineteenth century Champagne production had overtaken still wine production in the Champagne region.

Champagne Refinements

In Dom Pérignon's day, the yeast sediments that collected in the neck of the inverted bottles were removed just before the Champagne was served. The method of dégorgement required some skill and, even so, some yeast sediment remained, making the Champagne somewhat cloudy. In 1884, Armand Walfart invented the *à la glace* method of dégorgement that is used today (see Méthode Champenoise, p 60). Chilling the Champagne also subdued the bubbles, which meant that less liquid was lost upon popping the cork.

d'Orléans, Voltaire, Louis XV, England's George II, Lord Chesterfield, and Prime Minister William Pitt the Younger all coveted the expensive drink and helped it gain its elegant, exclusive, and sophisticated reputation. Even then, the cost of producing Champagne was steep due to the need for hand-blown bottles and the fact that breakage caused by the gas pressure could be as high as 50 percent.

During the nineteenth century Champagne production grew by leaps and bounds, and by 1853, ten million bottles were produced each year and exported all over Europe. Henriot (1808), Joseph Perrier (1825),

ABOVE AND OPPOSITE: Champagnes and sparkling wines should be refrigerated just prior to serving; prolonged exposure to cold temperatures will flatten the bubbles and hide the flavor.

Another improvement on Pérignon's methods was made by Nicole-Barbe Clicquot, who inherited her late husband's company in 1806. In order to avoid the unwanted collection of sediment along the sides of the bottles that resulted from simply laying the bottles horizontally, she had holes drilled into her kitchen table so that the bottles could be inverted but remain accessible to be given a twist every once in a while. Antoine Muller, her cellarmaster, came up with the crowning touch—cutting the holes at a perfect 45-degree angle. This meant that the bottles could start off horizontally to develop their bubbles, and gradually be tilted vertically each time they were twisted. By 1850 the use of these boards with angled holes, *pupitres*, had become the practice of choice in all Champagne houses.

Another problem that needed immediate attention was the high rate of breakage. This was not only economically undesirable, it was gravely dangerous to cellar workers. In 1836, Antoine François, a chemist, invented the *sucreoenomètre,* a device that measured the sugar level of the wine before second fermentation. He was able to devise a formula for calculating the correct amount of sugar to add in the *liqueur de tirage* to produce controlled levels of pressure. His work, in addition to the development of stronger glass bottles, lowered the bottle breakage rate from about 50 percent (and a startling 80 percent in the disastrous year of 1828) to the 0.5 percent that it is today.

Champagne in the Twentieth Century

Although Champagne's success was undeniable by the turn of the twentieth century, its popularity led to large-scale fraudulent production of "Champagne," which was made by pumping carbon dioxide into largely undistinguished still white wine. Born of necessity, the Comité Interprofessionnel du Vin de Champagne (CIVC) was formed in 1941 to protect wine growers, producers, and consumers. Although the CIVC has met with great success within Europe, sparkling wines not from the Champagne region may still be found labeled improperly as "Champagne" in Australia and North America.

Funded by both the Champagne growers and the Champagne houses, the CIVC is headed jointly by the president of the *vignerons*, the growers, and the president of the *negociants*, or houses. The presidents are assisted by the Commission Consultative, which is made up of an additional six growers and six houses. The CIVC is primarily concerned with keeping up a harmonious relationship between growers and houses, and managing their common interests, such as technical research and development, the growth of the Champagne market, the defense of the regional name, and public relations. The activity of the CIVC peaks at harvest time, when it makes recommendations as to when to start picking the grapes, what yield per hectare can be expected, and what the price should be. The organization is also responsible for supervising a very active three to four-week market for the exchange of grapes between Champagne growers and houses with impartiality and fairness.

Another twentieth-century problem was the devastation and setbacks that occurred when the vineyards of Champagne were attacked by phylloxera, a small, root-eating louse that had come from America in the 1860s. By the time the infestation reached Champagne in 1892, the curative method of grafting European vines onto resistant American rootstocks was well known. However, this was an arduous and expensive task, which

meant, essentially, that every grower had to start from scratch, as it was necessary to wait four years for the newly grafted vines to start producing. It took several decades before the process of grafting was fully completed.

Problems continued as World War I turned many vineyards into battlefields and greatly hurt production. Champagne slumped even further when the United States declared Prohibition in 1920 (the law was not repealed until 1933). World War II was less physically harmful to the region than the previous World War, but during the German occupation, one million bottles of Champagne had to be sent to the German troops every three weeks, and Champagne consumption by French civilians was banned. The CIVC was eventually successful in getting permission from the German authorities to sell one quarter of the Champagne production to civilians in France, Belgium, Sweden, and Finland, as well as securing the non-deportation of young men from Reims on the grounds

ABOVE: Most Champagnes are made of blends from several harvests. A mere 20% of Champagnes are vintage because the grape harvest is usually too small to produce Champagnes made solely from that year's bounty.

that they were needed to work in the cellars. The region was liberated by the surprise arrival of General Patton's 3rd Army on August 28, 1944. Rumor has it that the Americans came none too soon, as the Germans were supposedly planning to bomb many of the region's cellars before they would be forced to surrender.

After the war, Champagne production experienced a grand rebirth, and by 1989, 248 million bottles were being sold annualy and more than 87,500 acres (35,000 hectares) were in production.

Big Names for Tiny Bubbles

Steeped in the heritage of the region yet always ready to apply new technologies in the quest to make the best possible wine, the great Champagne houses exist as unique combinations of innovation and tradition. Each house has its own fascinating story; here are a few capsule histories of just some of the venerable Champagne makers.

Jacquesson & Fils

The House of Jacquesson was founded in 1798 by Memmie Jacquesson, who would later be joined by his son, Adolphe, to form Jacquesson & Fils. The Champagne that flowed from this house quickly became a favorite of Napoleon, who personally presented Jacquesson with a gold medal, then the highest honor for outstanding commercial enterprises, in 1810. In 1844, Adolphe came up with a crucial invention: a metal "capsule" and a wire "muselet," that even today, hold all Champagne corks securely in place.

A distinguishing feature of Jacquesson's Champagnes is that they are pressed in traditional wooden presses and fermented in oak barrels. The House produces the relatively small amount of 25,000 cases of wine each year, and has earned the reputation of producing Champagnes that are carefully made by hand and that meet the highest standards.

Bollinger

Champagne Bollinger was founded in 1829 in Aÿ, by Jacques Bollinger and his colleagues Paul Renaudin and the Comte de Villermont. This house is unique in that it is still family owned and run to this day. Champagne Bollinger is famous for using high percentages of Pinot Noir grapes and for extra aging on the lees, which encourages the yeasts to release their aromas for a richer flavor.

During a visit to *la Champagne* in 1788 Thomas Jefferson discovered what he called "the best Champagne," a 1783 vintage produced from grapes grown by M. Dorsay; Jefferson purchased his entire remaining stock. These same vineyards are now owned by Bollinger. Since then, Bollinger has received seven Royal Warrants from various members of the English royalty, from Queen Victoria in 1884 to Queen Elizabeth II in 1971.

The renowned Lily Bollinger took over the company after the death of her husband, Jacques, in 1941.

OPPOSITE: Pol Roger was Winston Churchill's favorite Champagne. In the early 1980s, Pol Roger decided to name its cuvée de prestige after him. The Cuvée Sir Winston Churchill is distinguishable by its black neck foil, commemorative of Churchill's death in 1965.

She led the house through the trying days of World War I (even pulling through a bombing raid in 1944). Lily retired from the company in 1972, leaving her nephew, Christian Bizot, in charge.

Pommery

In 1857 Louis Pommery, a wool trader, and his wife, Jeanne Alexandrine Melin, turned to the Champagne industry as the prospects of the wool trade dimmed. M. Pommery died just one year later and Jeanne Alexandrine took over the business. Madame Pommery was reputed to have been a creative and innovative woman with a solid education and business sense. Businessman Henry Vasnier joined forces with Madame Pommery, as well as Adolphe Hubinet, who assisted with sales and marketing.

Madame Pommery opened her own Champagne boutique in 1860 and launched a direct marketing and public relations campaign to introduce the new Champagne to the world. In 1874, in a clever response to the recognized English taste for lighter, less sweet Champagnes, Pommery Nature became the first brut in the history of Champagne.

Perrier-Jouët

Pierre Nicolas-Marie Perrier and Adele Jouët founded Perrier-Jouët in 1811 in the heart of *la Champagne*. The success of this husband-and-wife team is due in part to their revelation that using Chardonnay wines in assemblages lent special flavors and characteristics to their Champagnes.

Charles Perrier, their son, took over in 1854 when Pierre died. He was responsible for expanding distribution and popularizing Perrier-Jouët in England. His house also was the first to produce a true vintage Champagne made from the grapes of a single year's harvest, as well as a *brut cuvée*, made with grape juice from the first pressing. It was under his leadership that Armand Walfart developed the method of disgorging that involves freezing the sediment then ejecting the ice plug.

Champagne Widows

The "Champagne widows" are a phenomenon in the region. The most famous was undoubtedly La Veuve (The Widow) Clicquot; more recent was Madame Lily Bollinger, who ran her late husband's company for thirty years (1941–71). Less well known were Madame Veuve Pommery, Madam Laurent-Perrier, and Madame Olry Roederer. When their husbands died, these women not only assumed responsibility for their firms, but often expanded their holdings and sales.

LEFT: The pressure in a bottle of Champagne is approximately equal to that of a bus tire. OPPOSITE: Why wait for an occasion to indulge in a Champagne-and-caviar moment? Make any evening special with this sublime combination.

Mumm bought Perrier-Jouët in 1959, but provided that the operators at that time would continue to run the house as an independent company. Champagne Perrier-Jouët is noted for its art-nouveau designer bottles, beginning with Emile Gallé's unique Belle Epoque green bottle with a painted enamel design of anemones.

M u m m

Champagne Mumm was founded in 1827 by Peter Arnold de Mumm and Frederick Giesler, and is best known for Cordon Rouge, first released in 1876. Champagne Mumm introduced innovative techniques such as larger (12,000 liter) fermentation containers and temperature-controlled stainless steel tanks for the primary fermentation stage, ensuring consistency of quality.

The Mumm family was German and had never applied for French citizenship. So, even though they had been living in France and making their living in the Champagne business for over one hundred years, their house was confiscated by the French during World War I. The Dubonnet family purchased the business in 1920, keeping the name Mumm. Mumm de Cramant was introduced during this decade (though it was first created in 1882) and became an instant hit. It is made from 100 percent Chardonnay grapes from a single grand cru grown in Cramant in the Côte des Blancs, and is released only two years after it is made.

Champagne Styles

The different houses each have a distinctive style. While it is difficult to describe precisely the complex signature of each style, here is a general guide:

Light-Bodied: *Abelé, A. Charbaut et Fils, Demoiselle, De Saint-Gall, Duval-Leroy, Paul Goerg, Jacquesson et Fils, Lanson*

Light- to Medium-Bodied: *Ayala, Billecart-Salmon, J. Lasalle, Laurent-Perrier, G.H. Mumm, Bruno Paillard, Perrier-Jouët, Pommery, Ruinart, Taittinger, De Venoge, Nicolas Feuillate*

Medium-Bodied: *Charles Heidsieck, Delamotte, Deutz, Diebolt, Jacquart, Leclerc Briant, Moët et Chandon, Joseph Perrier, Philipponnat, Piper-Heidsieck, Pol Roger*

Medium- to Full-Bodied: *Paul Bara, Gaston Chiquet, Heidsieck-Monopole, Henriot, Serge Mathieu, Egly-Ouriet, Louis Roederer, Salon, J. Sélosse*

Full-Bodied: *Bollinger, Drappier, Gosset, Alfred Gratien, Krug, Tarlant, Veuve Clicquot*

Storing and Serving Champagne

Storing Champagne

Champagne is sold ready to drink and need not be aged further. However, certain connoisseurs believe that vintage sparkling wines should be aged for one to three years in a wine cellar, and that non-vintage sparkling wines should remain unopened for six to eight months in order to gain composure and harmony. Indeed, many importers allow their bottles to rest for six months before distributing them to retailers, letting the Champagne become settled, rounder, softer, and more complete. Old Champagnes, those aged for about ten years, are not at all harsh and have well-developed flavors and aromas. However, older sparkling wines tend to lose their sparkle very soon after being poured, and do not have the crispness or effervescence associated with Champagne.

Champagne should be consumed within a week or two of purchase, or stored in a cool, dark place. Bottles

RIGHT: Bottles are stored at 45° angles during refermentation.

exposed to sunlight and fluctuating temperatures will be irreversibly spoiled within a week or two. Make sure to store the bottles lying flat on their sides.

Serving Champagne

The old-fashioned wide Champagne glass is said to have been modeled on the breast of Marie-Antoinette, and was originally designed as a vessel for the non-sparkling wines of Champagne. It is a beautiful design no doubt, but a poor one for

sparkling wines. The large surface area causes the bubbles to release their gas and aromas rapidly, and the automatic urge to cradle the glass in the palm of the hand causes the wine to heat up.

The Champagne flute, a tall slender glass, is elegant as well as functional. The aromas are concentrated by the narrow opening of the glass, and the sparkling wine remains bubbly and nicely chilled.

Champagne should be chilled in the refrigerator for two to four hours, to a temperature of 42–47°F (5-8°C) before serving. In a pinch, half an hour in a bucket of ice and ice water should do the trick. Chilling Champagne makes it taste better and subdues the bubbles by quelling the pressure. If Champagne is too chilled, however, its flavor and bouquet will be muted.

When opening Champagne, always point the bottle away from your body, either upright or at a 45-degree angle, and avoid pointing it in anyone's direction. Put a thumb on the cork, and untwist and loosen the wire muzzle. Grasp the cork firmly, twist the bottle slowly and let the pressure help push out the cork. Champagne is best served by first pouring a little into each flute. After the initial foam subsides, top each glass to about half to two-thirds full.

For a Champagne aperitif at cocktail hour, allow one bottle for every three or four guests. A lesser Champagne or sparkling wine is often recommended for mixing combination drinks because the additions mask the subtleties of a truly fine wine—and why waste it? When served at a meal, count on one bottle for every two or three people. And for the traditional Champagne toast, one bottle can serve six to ten people.

OPPOSITE: A Champagne flute should be no more than two-thirds full.

A Perfect Union: Champagne & Caviar

Although one usually waits for a special occasion as an excuse to indulge in a service of Champagne and caviar, I say serving Champagne and caviar is a special occasion in itself. There have been scores of writers before me who have tried to capture the essence of this blissful pairing. They describe the magical interplay between the bursting pearly spheres of the salty caviar eggs and the sparkling frothy bubbles of the wine. They wax poetic about the constant tiny explosions of flavor in the mouth—first saline and piercing, then acidic and floral, and over and over until the caviar tin is depleted and the Champagne bottle drained of its wine.

Those most dedicated to the consumption of Champagne and caviar have definite opinions as to which eggs go with which sparkling wines. They say that they couldn't imagine nibbling a blini of bracing osetra with anything but a flute of vintage rosé, or a spoonful of creamy beluga without sips of an austere, bone-dry extra-brut.

I say that as long as there is enough good-quality caviar and Champagne on ice, there is almost nothing in the world that can spoil your party. Let that be your guide and you can do no wrong.

Buckwheat Blinis

Back in blini history, hot blinis were served by Russian street vendors during maslentisa, *the "butterweek" festival that took place the week prior to Lent. Melted butter, sour cream, herring, smoked sturgeon, salmon, whitefish, and, of course, caviar were the various accompaniments.*

Serves 6

- 1 ½ cups milk
- 1 ½ tablespoons sugar
- 2 ½ teaspoons active dry yeast
- 1 cup all-purpose flour
- ⅓ cup buckwheat flour
- 1 teaspoon salt
- 6 tablespoons butter
- 3 large eggs, lightly beaten
- Caviar for garnish

1. In a small saucepan, heat the milk until small bubbles appear around the edges of the pan. Remove the pan from the heat and stir in the sugar until dissolved. Cool the milk until it is just warm to the touch. Sprinkle in the yeast. Let stand for 5 minutes.

2. In a large bowl, combine the all-purpose flour, buckwheat flour, and salt. In a small saucepan, melt 4 tablespoons of the butter. Stir the milk mixture well and add it and the melted butter to the flour mixture. Mix until smooth. Cover the bowl with plastic wrap and let rise in a warm place until doubled in bulk, about 1½ hours.

3. When batter has risen, beat in eggs until smooth.

4. Preheat the oven to 200°F. Melt half the remaining butter in a nonstick skillet. When the foam subsides, form round blinis using 2 tablespoons of the batter for each. Cook the blinis on one side until bubbles appear on the top, then flip and cook for 1 to 2 minutes longer. Repeat with remaining batter, adding butter to the pan as needed. Keep the blinis warm in the oven, covered with foil, while cooking the remaining blinis.

Serve with a nutty vintage Champagne.

American Cornmeal Blinis

Made without yeast, these tender blinis have a true corn flavor. They are most appropriately served with American caviar, although any type is wonderful.

Serves 8

1 ¼ cups yellow cornmeal

¾ cup all-purpose flour

1 teaspoon baking powder

½ teaspoon salt

1 ⅔ cups half-and-half

4 tablespoons butter

2 large eggs

Caviar for garnish

1. In a large bowl, combine the cornmeal, flour, baking powder, and salt. Mix well. In a small saucepan, melt 2 tablespoons of the butter.

2. In another bowl, whisk together the half-and-half, the melted butter, and the eggs. Add the half-and-half mixture to the dry ingredients and mix just until smooth.

3. Preheat the oven to 200°F. Melt half the remaining butter in a nonstick skillet. When the foam subsides, form round blinis using 2 tablespoons of the batter for each. Cook the blinis on one side until bubbles appear on the top, then flip and cook for 1 to 2 minutes longer. Repeat with remaining batter, adding butter to the pan as needed. Keep the blinis warm in the oven, covered with foil, while cooking the remaining blinis.

Serve with a crisp Blanc de Blancs.

New Potatoes with Caviar and Crème Fraîche

Creamy, delicate crème fraîche or sour cream is the perfect foil for caviar. Place a dollop onto boiled new potato slices, top with your favorite roe (pressed caviar is a good choice), and you'll have very convenient and elegant little nibbles.

Serves 6 to 8

6 small new potatoes (about 1 pound)

½ cup crème fraîche or sour cream

3 to 4 ounces pressed or other caviar

Dill sprigs or phyllo sheets for garnish

1. Bring a large pot of water to a boil. Add the potatoes and cook until they are easily pierced with a knife, about 20 minutes. Drain and let cool.

2. Halve the potatoes, then slice off a bit of the rounded side of each half so they don't roll. Place them on a platter. Dollop a bit of the crème fraîche mixture on the potatoes, then top with a bit of the caviar. Garnish with shaved phyllo or dill sprigs and serve at once. For a variation, mix a tablespoon of minced fresh dill into the crème fraîche.

Serve with a light-style non-vintage Brut.

Smoked Salmon Mousse with Caviar

With mounds of pale pink mousse resting on green cucumber slices, garnished with beads of salmon or golden caviar, this makes an elegant and very beautiful hors d'oeuvre.

Serves 8

- ½ pound smoked salmon
- 1 cup heavy cream
- 4 ounces cream cheese, softened
- ¼ cup sour cream
- 1 tablespoon minced red onion
- 2 teaspoons fresh lemon juice
- 2 teaspoons chopped fresh dill
- White pepper, to taste
- 1 English (hothouse) cucumber, cut into ¼-inch rounds
- 2 ounces salmon or golden caviar

1. In the bowl of a food processor fitted with a steel blade, combine the smoked salmon, cream, cream cheese, sour cream, onion, and lemon juice. Process until very smooth, about 1½ minutes. Add the dill and white pepper and pulse to combine.

2. Using a pastry bag or a spoon, mound the salmon mousse onto the cucumber slices. Top with the caviar and serve at once.

Serve with a crisp-style Brut.

Borscht

A traditional Russian favorite, borscht's brilliant color is emphasized
by the sour cream and caviar garnish.

Serves 4

6 medium beets

6 cups beef or chicken stock

1 cup sour cream

Caviar and dill for garnish

1. Peel the beets and cut into quarters. Place them in a large pot with the stock and bring to a boil. Remove from the pot when soft.

2. Divide the cooked beets in half. Using a food processor, puree half the beets; julienne the remaining half.

3. Place a portion of julienned beet in the center of each bowl; pour the pureed beet on top. The julienned portion will rise to the top.

4. Place a dollop of sour cream and caviar atop the mound of julienne; garnish with dill.

Serve with a Blanc de Noirs.

Fresh Tagliatelle with Chives, Crème Fraîche, and Salmon Caviar

Pasta and caviar may seem an unlikely couple, but this creamy pasta comes alive with the addition of the tangy salmon roe.

Serves 6

1 pound fresh tagliatelle

³/₄ cup crème fraîche

3 tablespoons butter

¹/₄ cup minced chives

6 ounces salmon caviar

Freshly ground black pepper, to taste

1. Cook the pasta in salted boiling water according to the package directions. Drain well and return to the pot. Add the crème fraîche and butter and toss until the butter is melted. Add the chives and toss to combine. Divide the pasta between six plates.

2. Top each portion of pasta with about an ounce of caviar and grind on some pepper. Serve immediately.

Serve with a medium-bodied non-vintage Brut.

Tuna Tartare with Wasabi Caviar on Taro Chips

Wasabi caviar (flying fish roe flavored with wasabi) adds zing to the tuna tartare; for a less fiery garnish, try using a sturgeon roe.

Serves 6

- ½ pound fresh, sushi-quality tuna
- 2 tablespoons minced scallion
- 1 tablespoon sesame oil
- 1 teaspoon soy sauce
- Salt and freshly ground black pepper, to taste
- Prepared taro chips (available in most large supermarkets)
- 2 ounces wasabi caviar

1. Using a large, sharp knife (not a food processor), mince the tuna and place it in a bowl. Add the scallion, sesame oil, soy sauce, salt, and pepper and toss well. Refrigerate the mixture for at least 2 hours to allow the flavors to blend.

2. When ready to serve, spoon some of the tartare onto each taro chip and garnish with the caviar. Serve immediately.

Serve with a Demi-Sec Champagne.

Phyllo Cups with Avocado, Mango, and Papaya

This tropical delight gets a welcome salty contrast from its caviar garnish.

Makes 15-20 cups, serves six as an appetizer

1 mango

1 papaya

1 avocado

1 small onion

Juice of 1 lime

20 premade phyllo cups

Caviar for garnish

1. Peel and finely chop the mango, papaya, avocado and onion.

2. Mix ingredients together and squeeze lime juice in.

3. Place a spoonful of the mixture into each phyllo cup and top with caviar.

Serve with a rosé Champagne.

Mail Order Sources

Prices listed are for 1-ounce containers of caviar in the order of: beluga, osetra, sevruga, unless otherwise indicated. All prices are current as of May, 1999. For small orders, you can expect to pay an additional $20-$25 for overnight shipping.

Balducci's
(800) 225-3822
(1oz.) $45, (2.5oz.) $75, (2.5oz.) $55
$20 overnight shipping charge

Caviar Direct
(800) 650-2828
fax (516) 767-8762
(2oz.) $90, $59, $39
Delivery available in NYC; $20 Fedex
    overnight elsewhere

Caviar Russe
Caspian Star Caviar, Inc.
(800) 2-CAVIAR
fax (718) 643-2640
$29.50, $15, $13.75
American sturgeon: $8.50 per 1oz.
$25 Fedex overnight shipping charge

Caviarteria
(800) 4-CAVIAR
fax (718) 482-8985
$58, $34, $33
American sturgeon: $55 per 3.5oz.
$20 overnight shipping charge

Dean & Deluca
(800) 221-7714
(2oz.) $95, $70, $65
$20 overnight shipping charge

Petrossian Boutique
(212) 245-2217
$75, $45, $35
$12.50 delivery in NYC; $25 Fedex
    overnight elsewhere

Russ & Daughters
(212) 475-4880
(1.75oz.) $69.95, $49.95, $39.95
$95 sampler contains 1oz. each beluga,
    osetra and sevruga
Delivery in NYC; $20-25 overnight
    elsewhere

Zabar's
(212) 787-2000
(2oz.) $55, $37, $33
$22 delivery in NYC; $25 Fedex overnight
    elsewhere

Index

Credits

The caviar in this book was supplied by Caviarteria. Look for them on the web at Caviarteria.com or call 1-800-4CAVIAR.

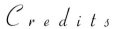

Principal Photography ©Bill Milne, with prop styling by Sylvia Lachter.

Food styling on pages 10, 14, 52, 95, 99, 100, 103, 105, 106, 108 by Nir Adar

Props Courtesy Galileo, NY; Carole Stupell Ltd. NY

Additional photography:
Corbis: ©Michael Busselle: 73; ©Marc Garanger: 58; ©Charles O'rear: 64, 65; ©Carl Purcell: 70

Corbis/Bettmann: 80

Envision: ©Agence Top: 23; ©Kenneth Chen: 13; ©Daryl J. Solomon: 86

Foodpix: 30-31; ©Bryan Hagawara: 39; ©Gentyl & Hyers: 3; ©Brian Leatart: 50; ©Penina: 96

Tony Stone Images: ©Joe Cornish: 89; ©James Harrington: 59; ©John Higginson: 56; ©Herb Schmitz: 63; ©Pete Seaward: 92; ©Vera Storman: 76

Photographs on pages 4, 9, 19, 29, 35, 49 shot on location at Caviarteria, 310 West Broadway, New York, NY 10013

Photographs on pages 6, 66–67, 87 shot on location at Canal House, Soho Grand Hotel, 310 West Broadway, New York, NY 10013

Approximate Metric Equivalents

1/4 teaspoon	=	1ml	1 oz.	=	30g	325°F	=	160°C
1/2 teaspoon	=	2ml	4 oz.	=	120g	350°F	=	180°C
3/4 teaspoon	=	3ml	8 oz.	=	240g	375°F	=	190°C
1 teaspoon	=	5ml	12 oz.	=	360g	400°F	=	200°C
1 tablespoon	=	15ml	16oz.	=	480g	425°F	=	220°C
1/4 cup	=	60ml				450°F	=	230°C
1/2 cup	=	120ml						
1 cup	=	240ml						
1 pint	=	480ml						
1 quart	=	960ml						